Disney
PRINCESS

Forever a Princess

The stories of
Aurora and Ariel

retold by Sue Kassirer

Reader's Digest
Children's Books®

Pleasantville, New York • Montréal, Québec • Bath, United Kingdom

Aurora

Once Upon a Dream

✦ ✦✖✦ ✦✖✦ ✦✖✦ ✦✖✦ ✦✖✦ ✦✖✦ ✦✖✦ ✦ ✦

Once upon a time, in a far-away land, lived a happy little child who didn't know she was a princess. *I* was that child.

Three kind women raised me in a tidy little cottage in the woods. Little did I know that they were really fairies, who had rescued me from the evil fairy Maleficent's dark curse.

As I grew older, I dreamed of meeting a tall, handsome stranger and falling in love. One day, my dream came true. As I walked through the woods on my sixteenth birthday, there he was. It was love at first sight!

But when I told the kind women the good news, they gasped. "You cannot marry him. For you are really a princess— Princess Aurora. And you were promised at birth to Prince Phillip!"

I dressed in a royal gown and wept as they whisked me off to the castle, my rightful home.

There, Maleficent tricked me into going
up into a high tower, where a spinning wheel
glowed in the darkness.

I pricked my finger
on the spindle, and was
soon sound asleep....

And there I slept until the magical day
when Prince Phillip arrived. Bending down, he
gave me a kiss of true love that broke the spell.

When I opened my eyes, I saw the stranger I had met in the woods. It turned out that he was Prince Phillip all along. And we lived happily ever after.

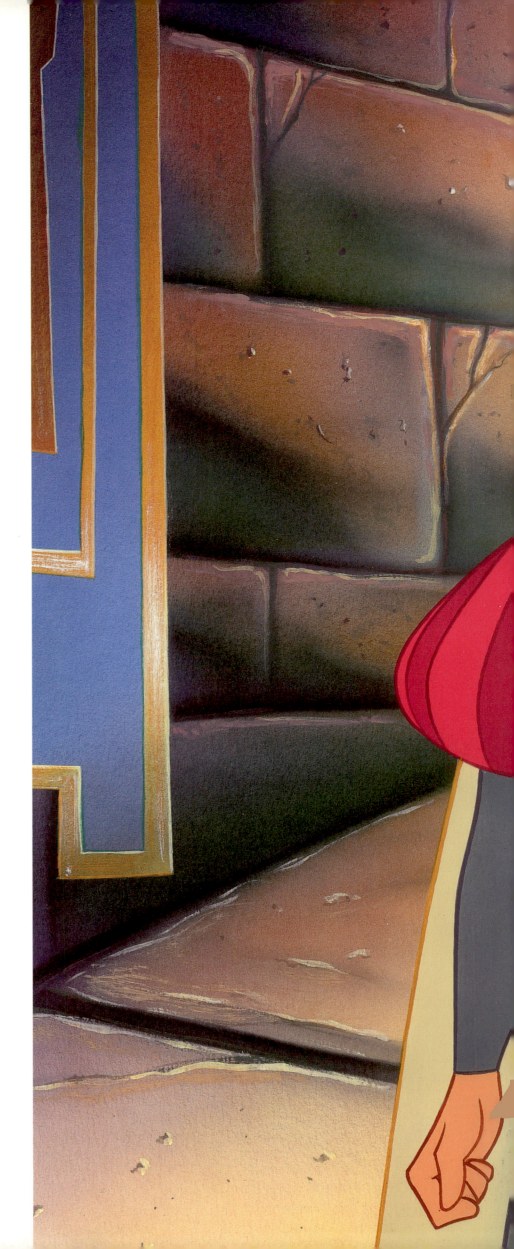

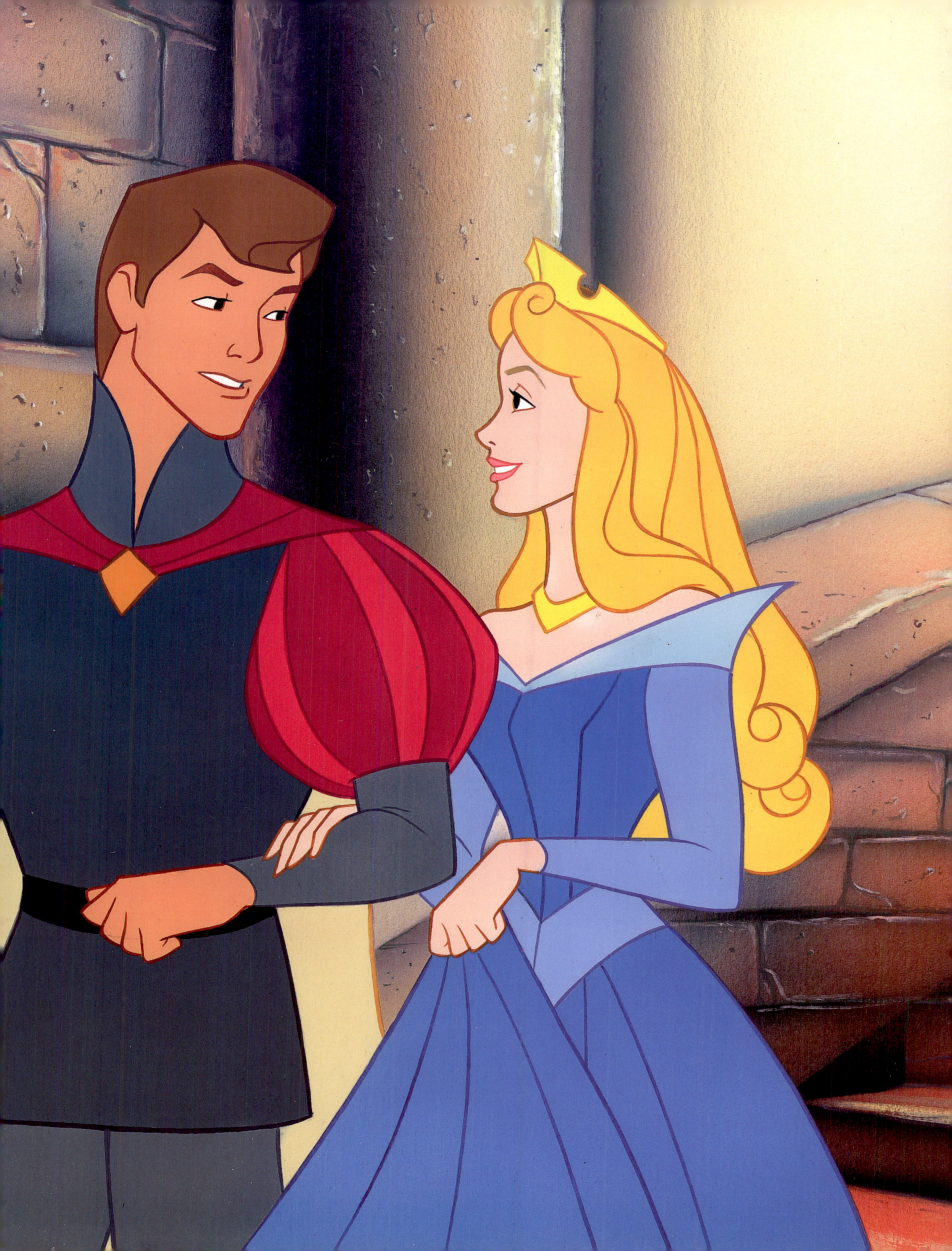

Ariel

Follow Your Dream

All my life I had lived under the beautiful sea. But even as a little girl I was fascinated by the land and by humans. Other than singing, human-watching was my favorite pastime.

I'll never forget the first time I saw him. There I was, peering over the deck of a ship—and Prince Eric appeared. It was love at first sight.

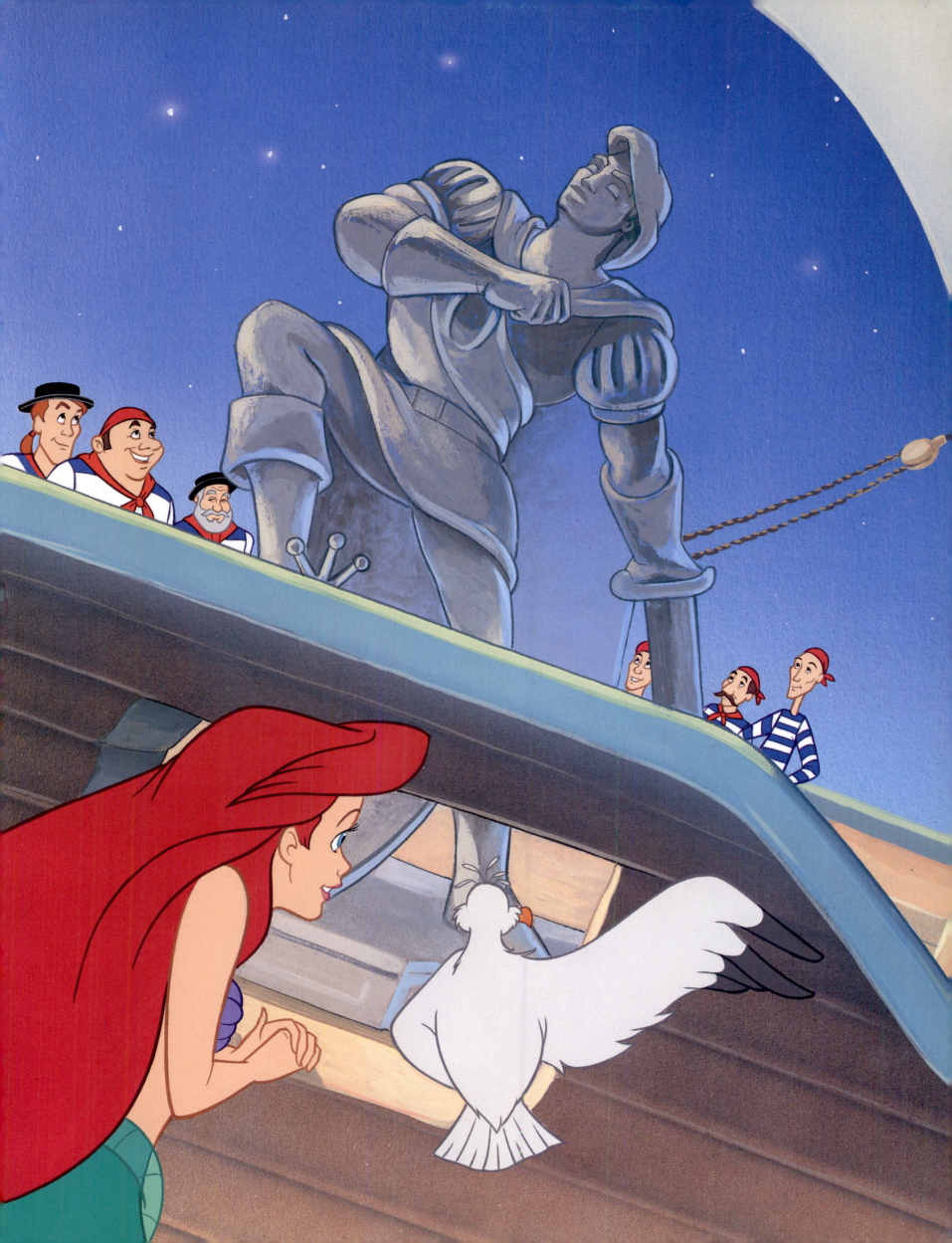

Suddenly, a storm began to rage and lightning hit the ship. Prince Eric was knocked overboard! Diving down deep, I pulled him to the surface. I saved his life!

When my father, King Triton, found out, he was furious. He told me to never go near humans again!

But I was truly lovesick. I went to see Ursula, the sea witch, who offered to turn me into a human. If, in three days, I could get Eric to kiss me, I would remain human. But if he *didn't* kiss me, I would turn back into a mermaid and belong to Ursula forever!

In return, I agreed to give Ursula my beautiful voice. As I sang, my voice flowed into a seashell locket. I could no longer speak.

For three days I tried to get the prince to kiss me. Every day he came closer...and closer. But each time, something went wrong. If only I could talk, or enchant him with my singing!

On the third day, I heard that Prince Eric was getting married—to someone named Vanessa! She had enchanted the prince with her golden voice. It turned out that Vanessa was really Ursula! And of course, the voice was really *my* voice.

When all my sea and bird friends
heard this, they rushed to the wedding
and attacked Vanessa. Her locket crashed
to the ground and out flew my voice,
which magically returned to me.

When the prince heard me speak, he knew that it was me he loved. From that day on, we have lived most happily ever after.

How to use this book

Now that you've met Aurora and Ariel, help them look glamorous as they prepare for the royal ball. They are depending on you to make them look dazzling.

• Carefully press out all purses and magnetic dresses for each princess.

• Now it's time to try some dresses on! The dolls and dresses are magnetic, so you just need to position them on the doll and they'll stay.

• Are you ready to make the dress even more dazzling? Use the jewels and stickers to make it look extra-special!

• Don't forget the accessory stickers! An elegant outfit is not complete without a pretty necklace, crown, or bouquet of flowers.

• To make your doll stand up, assemble the base as shown in figure on right.

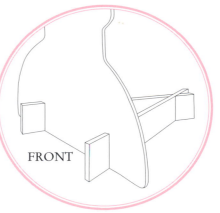

FRONT

• When you are finished playing, carefully remove the jewels and stickers from the doll and store them on the back cover of your book.